FINGERPICKING
GOSPEL

T0082985

2   DOWN AT THE CROSS (GLORY TO HIS NAME)

4   HIGHER GROUND

6   HIS EYE IS ON THE SPARROW

9   JESUS IS THE SWEETEST NAME I KNOW

10 JUST A CLOSER WALK WITH THEE

12 LOVE LIFTED ME

14 NEARER, MY GOD, TO THEE

16 THE OLD RUGGED CROSS

18 PRECIOUS MEMORIES

20 SHALL WE GATHER AT THE RIVER?

22 SWEET BY AND BY

24 TURN YOUR EYES UPON JESUS

26 WAYFARING STRANGER

28 WHEN WE ALL GET TO HEAVEN

30 WILL THE CIRCLE BE UNBROKEN

32 INTRODUCTION TO FINGERSTYLE GUITAR

ISBN 978-1-4234-6877-6

HAL•LEONARD®
CORPORATION
7777 W. BLUEMOUND RD. P.O. BOX 13819 MILWAUKEE, WI 53213

In Australia Contact:
Hal Leonard Australia Pty. Ltd.
4 Lentara Court
Cheltenham, Victoria, 3192 Australia
Email: ausadmin@halleonard.com.au

Visit Hal Leonard Online at
www.halleonard.com

Down at the Cross
(Glory to His Name)

Words by Elisha A. Hoffman
Music by John H. Stockton

Drop D tuning:
(low to high) D-A-D-G-B-E

Verse
Moderately

1. Down at the cross where my Sav - ior died,
2., 3., 4. *See additional lyrics*

down where for cleans - ing from sin I cried, there to my heart was the

blood ap - plied; glo - ry to His name!

Chorus

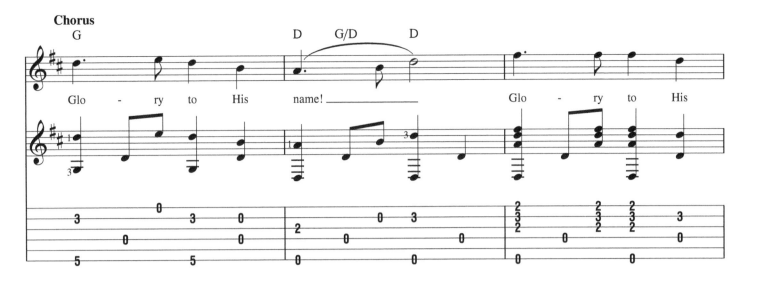

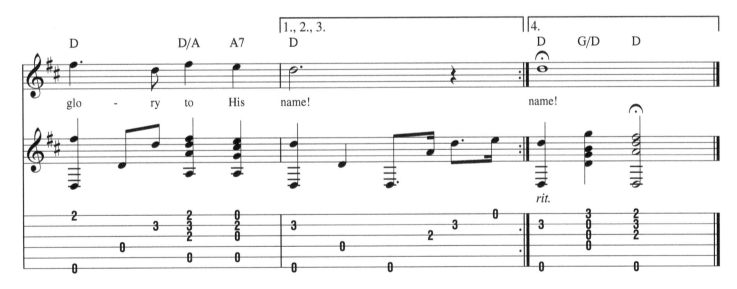

Additional Lyrics

2. I am so wondrously saved from sin,
   Jesus so sweetly abides within.
   There at the cross where He took me in;
   Glory to His name!

3. O precious fountain that saves from sin,
   I am so glad I have entered in;
   There Jesus saves me and keeps me clean;
   Glory to His name!

4. Come to this fountain so rich and sweet,
   Cast thy poor soul at the Savior's feet.
   Plunge in today and be made complete;
   Glory to His name!

Higher Ground

Words by Johnson Oatman, Jr.
Music by Charles H. Gabriel

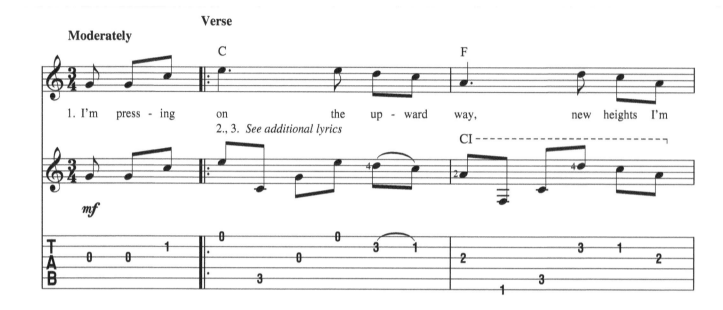

1. I'm press - ing on the up - ward way, new heights I'm
2., 3. *See additional lyrics*

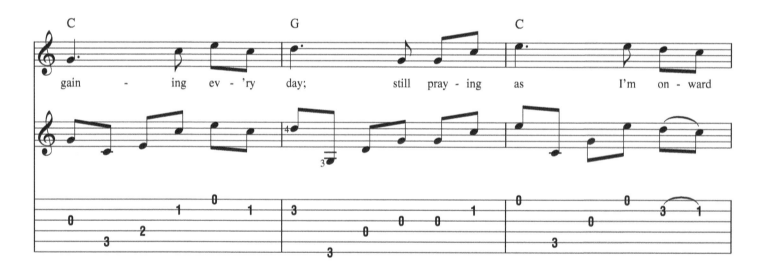

gain - ing ev - 'ry day; still pray - ing as I'm on - ward

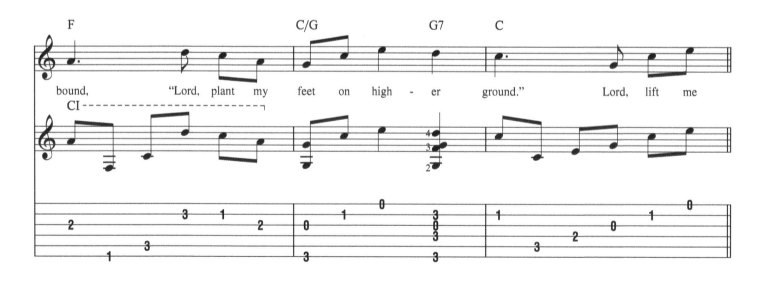

bound, "Lord, plant my feet on high - er ground." Lord, lift me

Chorus

up and let me stand, by faith, on heav - en's ta - ble

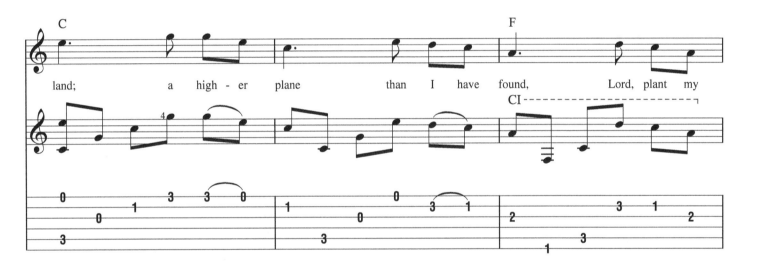

land; a high - er plane than I have found, Lord, plant my

feet on high - er ground.
2. I want to ground.
3. I want to

Additional Lyrics

2. I want to live above the world,
   Though Satan's darts at me are hurled;
   For faith has caught the joyful sound,
   The song of saints on higher ground.

3. I want to scale the utmost height,
   And catch a gleam of glory bright;
   But still I'll pray till heav'n I've found,
   "Lord, lead me on to higher ground."

His Eye Is on the Sparrow

Words by Civilla D. Martin
Music by Charles H. Gabriel

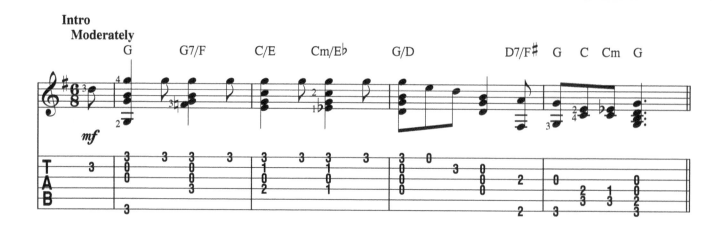

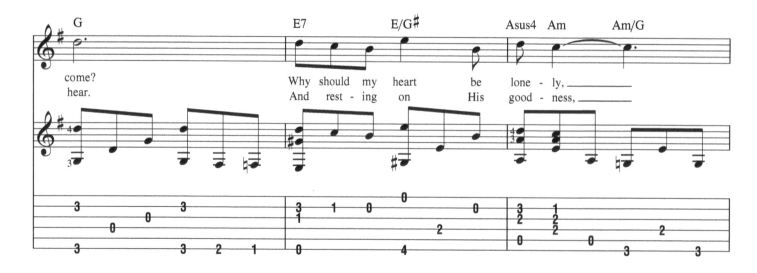

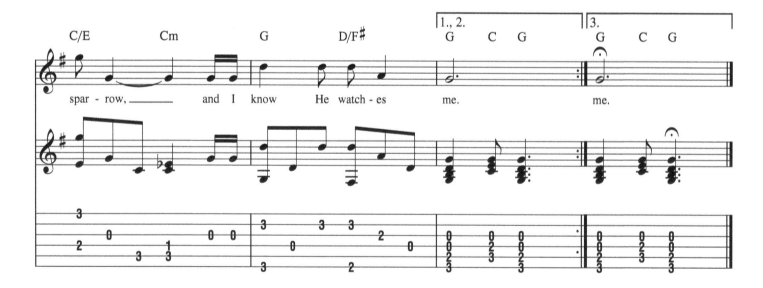

Additional Lyrics

3. Whenever I am tempted, whenever clouds arise,
   When song gives place to sighing, when hope within me dies.
   I draw the closer to Him, from care He sets me free.

Jesus Is the Sweetest Name I Know

Words and Music by Lela Long

Just a Closer Walk With Thee

Traditional
Arranged by Kenneth Morris

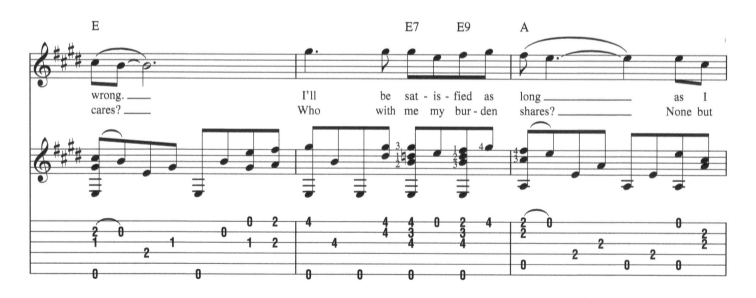

Love Lifted Me

Words by James Rowe
Music by Howard E. Smith

I was sink - ing deep in sin, far from the peace - ful

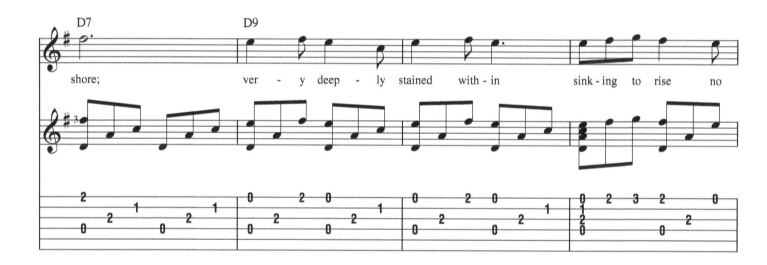

shore; ver - y deep - ly stained with - in sink - ing to rise no

more. But the Mas - ter of the sea heard my des - pair - ing

Nearer, My God, to Thee

Words by Sarah F. Adams
Based on Genesis 28:10-22
Music by Lowell Mason

Drop D tuning:
(low to high) D-A-D-G-B-E

Verse
Moderately

1. Near - er, my God, to Thee, near -
2. – 5. *See additional lyrics*

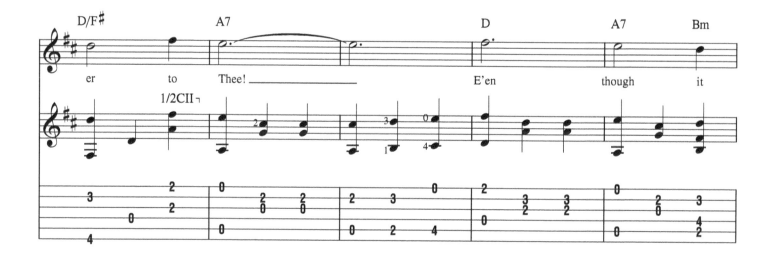

er to Thee! _____ E'en though it

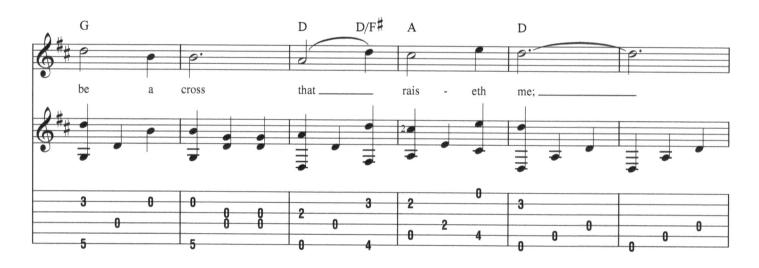

be a cross that _____ rais - eth me;

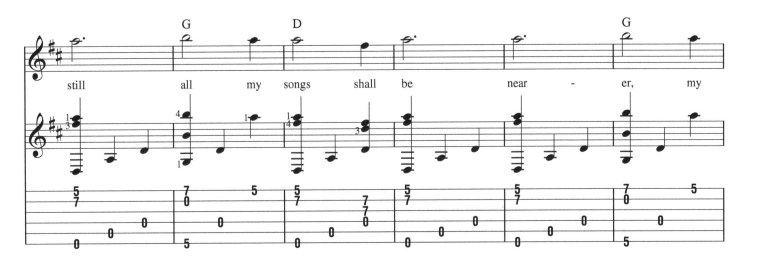

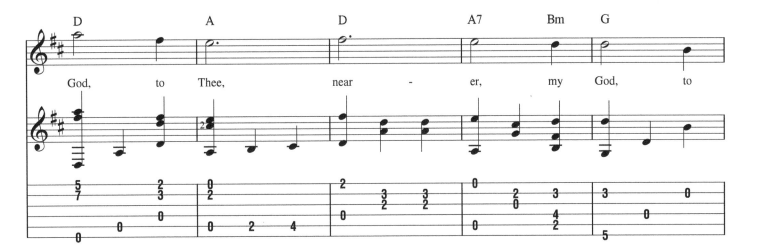

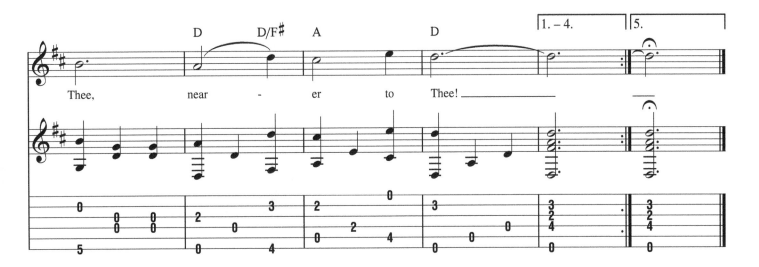

Additional Lyrics

2. Though like the wanderer, the sun gone down;
   Darkness be over me, my rest a stone.
   Yet in my dreams I'll be nearer, my God, to Thee,
   Nearer, my God, to Thee, nearer to Thee.

3. There let the way appear, steps unto heav'n;
   All that Thou sendest me in mercy giv'n.
   Angels to beckon me nearer, my God, to Thee,
   Nearer, my God, to Thee, nearer to Thee.

4. Then, with my waking thoughts bright with my praise,
   Out of my stony griefs, Bethel I'll raise.
   So by my woes to be nearer, my God, to Thee,
   Nearer, my God, to Thee, nearer to Thee.

5. Or if on joyful wing, cleaving the sky,
   Sun, moon, and stars forgot; upward I'll fly,
   Still all my songs shall be nearer, my God, to Thee,
   Nearer, my God, to Thee, nearer to Thee.

The Old Rugged Cross

Words and Music by Rev. George Bennard

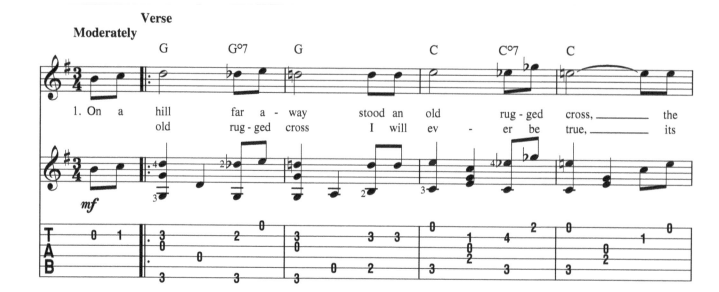

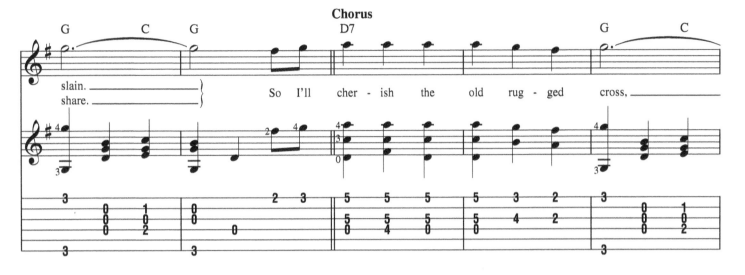

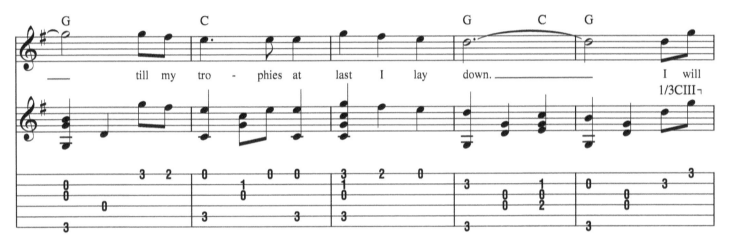

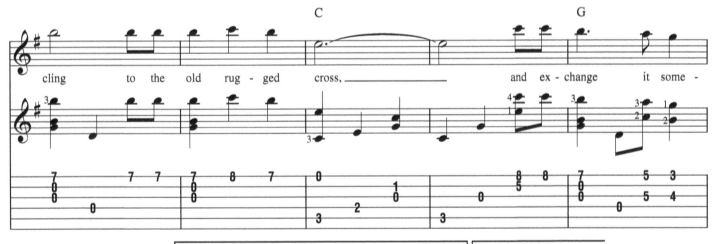

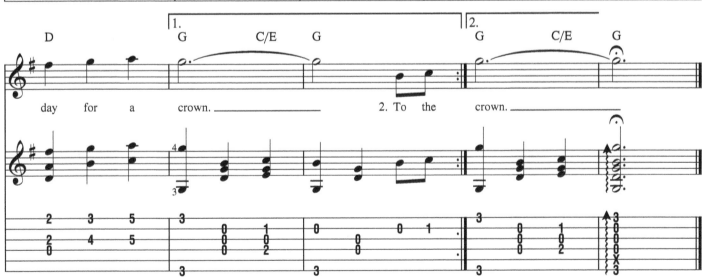

Precious Memories

Words and Music by J.B.F. Wright

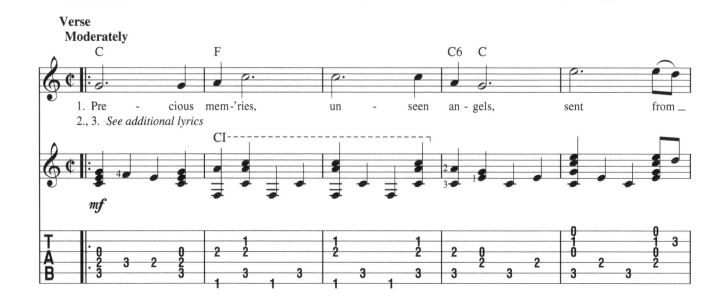

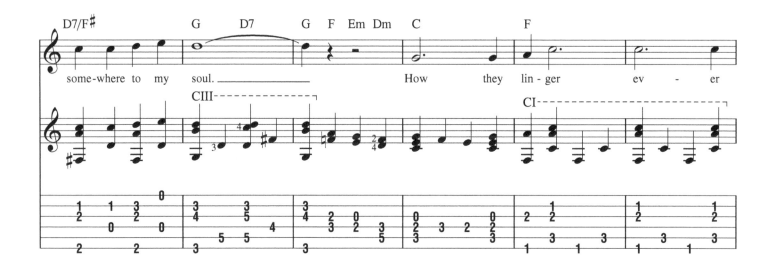

Chorus

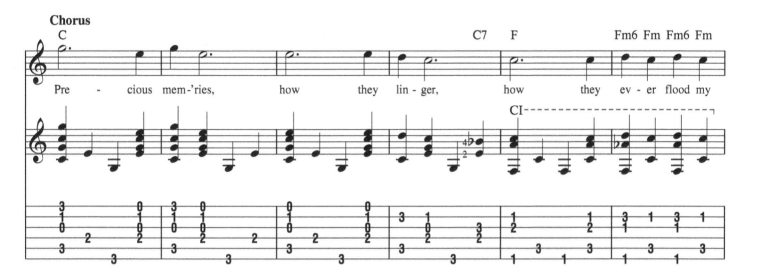

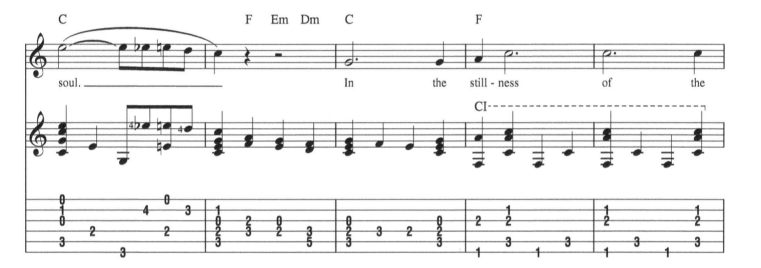

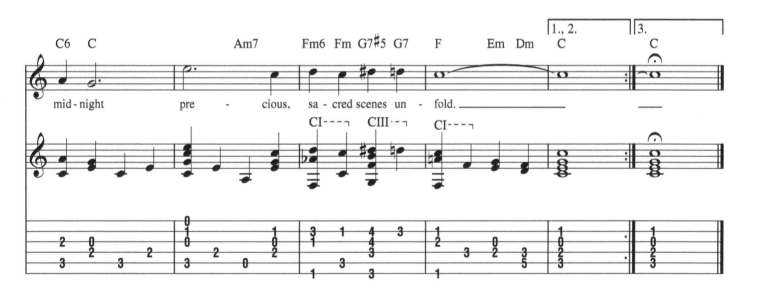

Additional Lyrics

2. Precious father, loving mother, fly across the lonely years
   To old home scenes of my childhood, with fond mem'ries appear.

3. As I travel on life's pathway, I know what life shall hold.
   As I wander hopes grow fonder. Precious mem'ries flood my soul.

Shall We Gather at the River?

Words and Music by Robert Lowry

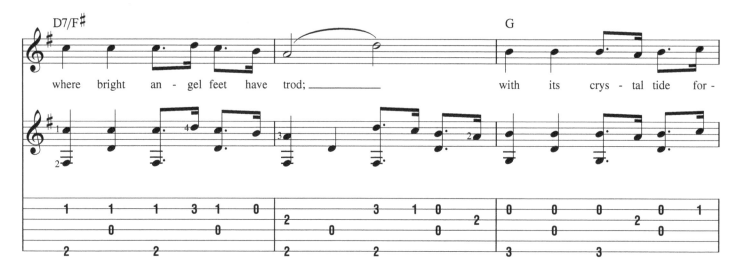

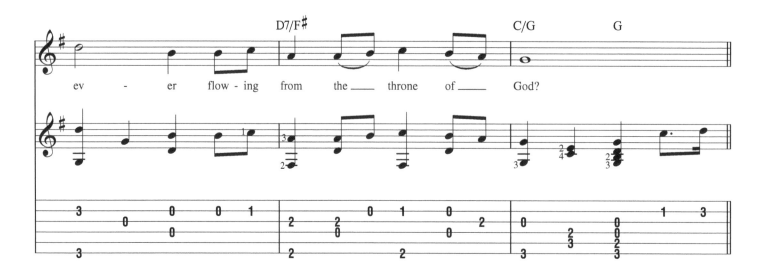

Chorus

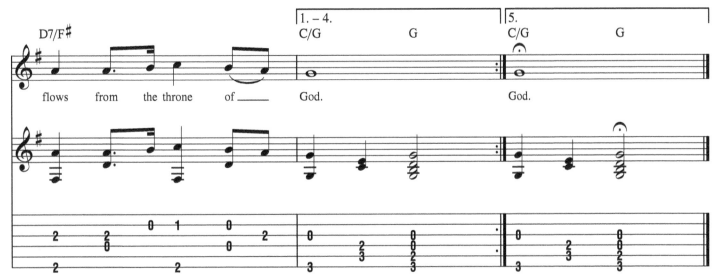

Additional Lyrics

2. On the margin of the river,
   Washing up its silver spray,
   We shall walk and worship ever,
   All the happy, golden day.

3. On the bosom of the river,
   Where the Savior King we own,
   We shall meet and sorrow never
   'Neath the glory of the throne.

4. Ere we reach the shining river,
   Lay we ev'ry burden down;
   Grace our spirits will deliver
   And provide a robe and crown.

5. Soon we'll reach the shining river,
   Soon our pilgrimage will cease.
   Soon our happy hearts will quiver
   With the melody of peace.

Sweet By and By

Words by Sanford Fillmore Bennett
Music by Joseph P. Webster

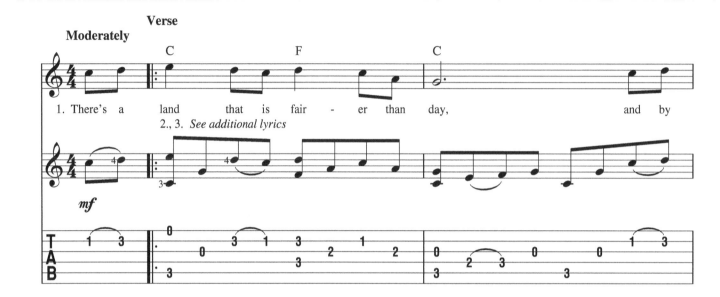

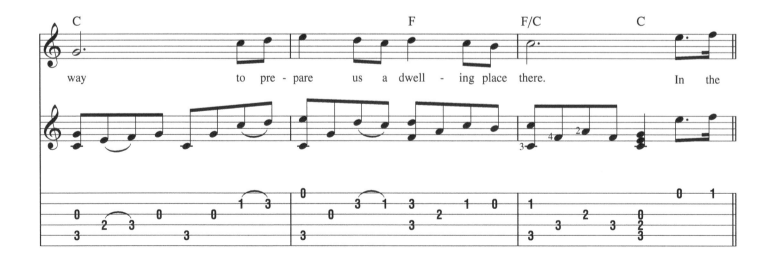

Chorus

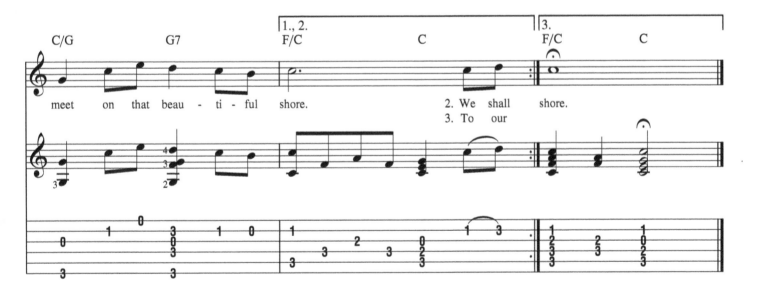

Additional Lyrics

2. We shall sing on that beautiful shore
   The melodious songs of the blessed;
   And our spirits shall sorrow no more,
   Not a sigh for the blessing of rest.

3. To our bountiful Father above,
   We will offer our tribute of praise
   For the glorious gift of His love
   And the blessings that hallow our days.

Turn Your Eyes Upon Jesus

Words and Music by Helen H. Lemmel

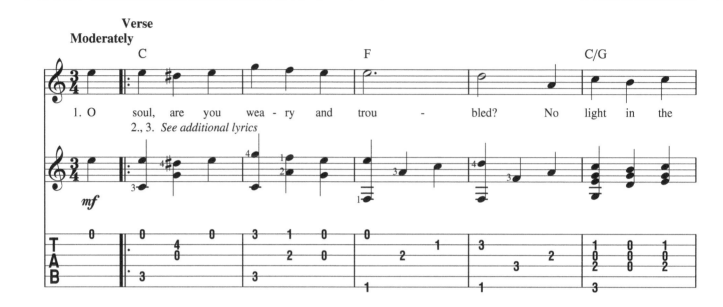

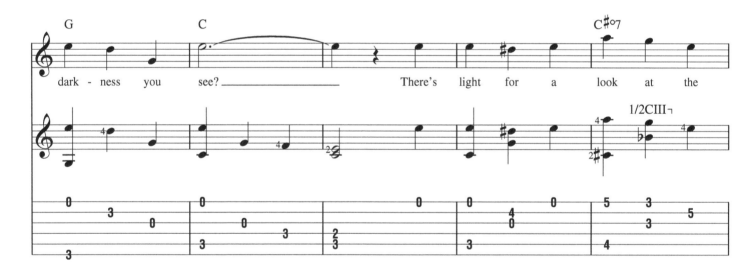

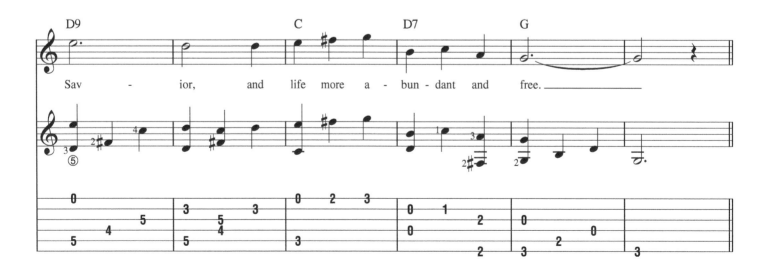

Chorus

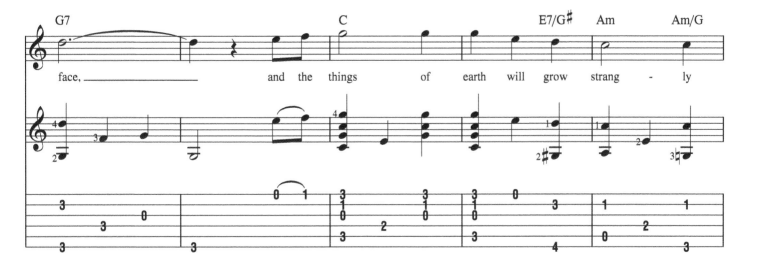

Additional Lyrics

2. Through death into life everlasting
He passed, and we follow Him there;
O'er us sin no more hath dominion
For more than conquerors we are!

3. His word shall not fail you He promised;
Believe Him, and all will be well.
Then go to a world that is dying,
His perfect salvation to tell!

Wayfaring Stranger

Southern American Folk Hymn

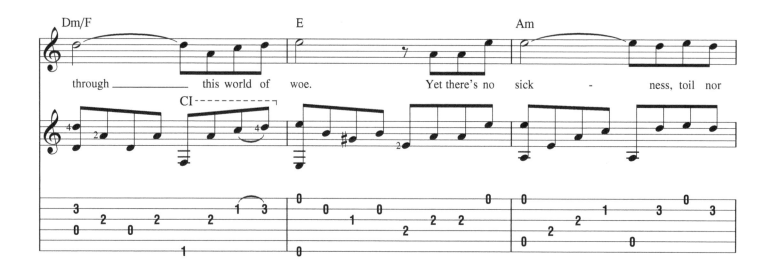

Additional Lyrics

2. I know dark clouds will gather 'round me,
   I know my way is rough and steep;
   But golden fields lie out before me
   Where God's redeemed shall ever sleep.
   I'm going there to see my mother;
   She said she'd meet me when I come.
   I'm only going over Jordan,
   I'm only going over home.

3. I'll soon be free from ev'ry trial,
   My body sleep in the church yard;
   I'll drop the cross of self-denial
   And enter on my great reward.
   I'm going there to see my Savior
   To sing His praise forevermore.
   I'm only going over Jordan,
   I'm only going over home.

When We All Get to Heaven

Words by Eliza E. Hewitt
Music by Emily D. Wilson

Verse
Moderately

1. Sing the won - drous love _____ of _____ Je - sus;
2., 3., 4. *See additional lyrics*

sing His mer - cy _____ and His grace. In the man - sions,

bright and bless - ed, He'll pre - pare for us a place. When we

Chorus

all ... get to heav - en, what a day of re - joic - ing that will

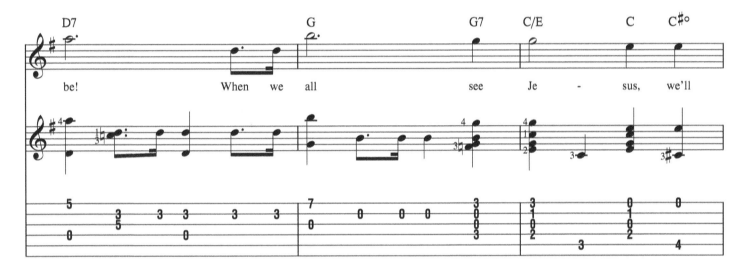

be! When we all see Je - sus, we'll

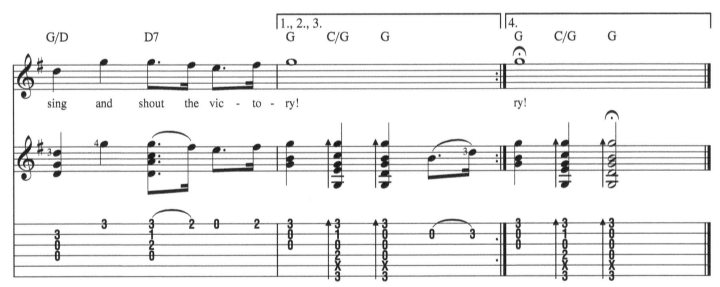

sing and shout the vic - to - ry! ry!

Additional Lyrics

2. While we walk the pilgrim pathway,
   Clouds will overspread the sky;
   But when trav'ling days are over,
   Not a shadow, not a sigh.

3. Let us then be true and faithful,
   Trusting, serving ev'ry day;
   Just one glimpse of Him in glory
   Will the toils of life repay.

4. Onward to the prize before us!
   Soon His beauty we'll behold;
   Soon the pearly gates will open;
   We shall tread the streets of gold.

Will the Circle Be Unbroken

Words by Ada R. Habershon
Music by Charles H. Gabriel

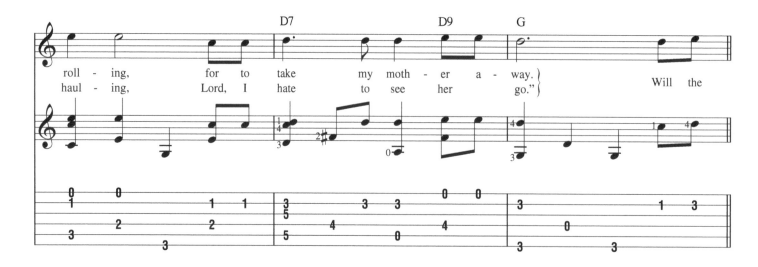

Chorus

cir - cle   be un - bro - ken,   by and by,   Lord, by and

by?   There's a bet - ter   home a - wait - ing   in the

sky,   in the sky.   2. Oh, I   sky.
                                     3. I will

Additional Lyrics

3. I will follow close behind her,
   Try to hold up and be brave.
   But I could not hide my sorrow,
   When they laid her in the grave.

INTRODUCTION TO FINGERSTYLE GUITAR

Fingerstyle (a.k.a. fingerpicking) is a guitar technique that means you literally pick the strings with your right-hand fingers and thumb. This contrasts with the conventional technique of strumming and playing single notes with a pick (a.k.a. flatpicking). For fingerpicking, you can use any type of guitar: acoustic steel-string, nylon-string classical, or electric.

THE RIGHT HAND

The most common right-hand position is shown here.

Use a high wrist; arch your palm as if you were holding a ping-pong ball. Keep the thumb outside and away from the fingers, and let the fingers do the work rather than lifting your whole hand.

The thumb generally plucks the bottom strings with downstrokes on the left side of the thumb and thumbnail. The other fingers pluck the higher strings using upstrokes with the fleshy tip of the fingers and fingernails. The thumb and fingers should pluck one string per stroke and not brush over several strings.

Another picking option you may choose to use is called hybrid picking (a.k.a. plectrum-style fingerpicking). Here, the pick is usually held between the thumb and first finger, and the three remaining fingers are assigned to pluck the higher strings.

THE LEFT HAND

The left-hand fingers are numbered 1 through 4.

Be sure to keep your fingers arched, with each joint bent; if they flatten out across the strings, they will deaden the sound when you fingerpick. As a general rule, let the strings ring as long as possible when playing fingerstyle.

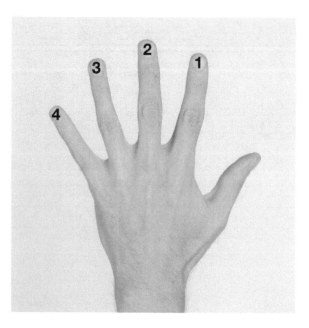